"What's up Doc?"
Interpreting in the Medical, Mental and allied Health Care Settings

Proceedings of the 25th efsli Conference
Toulouse, France, 9th-10th September 2017

European Forum of Sign Language Interpreters
2018

efsli 2017 proceedings

ISBN 9789090311630
© European Forum of Sign Language Interpreters, 2018
Edited by: Sandra Pratt, Thaisa Whistance
efsli editing coordinator: Marianna Hatzopoulou
efsli post-editing by: Marinella Salami
Cover design: Triin Jõeveer
Cover photos: ©magena360
Printed by: *Createspace*

This publication is made possible with the support of the Erasmus Plus Programme. The European Commission support for the production of this publication does not constitute endorsement of the contents which reflect the views only of the authors, and the Commission cannot be held responsible for any use which may be made of the information contained therein.

All rights reserved

No part of this publication may be produced, stored in a retrieval system or transmitted in any form or any means (electronic, photocopying, recording or otherwise), without the prior written permission of the publisher.

efsli 2017 proceedings

Table of Contents

efsli President's Foreword..............................6
Ivana Bućko

Presentations

A multi-disciplinary approach to interpreting – improving communication by training medical students..................8
Paul Belmonte and Shaurna Dickson

The internal representations used by Sign Language Interpreters in the healthcare settings: description and didactic activities...16
Dr. Rayco H. González Montesino

The use of Situated Learning in the training of Sign Language Interpreters working in Healthcare domains...35
Thaïsa Hughes and Sarah Bown

Sign Language in Worldwide Medicine 53
Dr Jean Dragon

Diagnosing Healthcare Assignments: Medical Interpreting for Deaf People in Europe................................. 56
Patricia Brück, Britta Meinicke, Juliane Rode

efsli President's Foreword

The 25th Conference of the European Forum of Sign Language Interpreters (efsli) was held in Toulouse, 9th-10th September 2017, and addressed an important topic for our profession: interpreting in medical, mental and allied health care settings.
The right to receive fair, dignified and equitable medical treatment is a fundamental human right; to ensure that individuals belonging to minority language communities gain this is a shared responsibility. Even so, we live in a Europe of varying speeds, where the country we live in matters in terms of accessibility and recognition of language and interpreting needs.

A total of 14 presentations (workshops, TED talks and parallel sessions) and 7 posters were presented during the conference. A wide range of scholars and practitioners shared their experiences and reflected on best practices.
These Proceedings include a selection of papers presented at the 2017 efsli conference exploring interpreting in those specialised settings from different perspectives. I am sure that these Proceedings will intensify knowledge sharing among professionals across Europe.

On behalf of efsli, I would like to express my gratitude to:

- the French Association of Sign Language Interpreters (AFILS) for hosting the conference;
- our keynote speaker, Colin Allen, President of the World Federation of the Deaf (WFD), and all presenters for their precious contributions;
- conference participants for their enthusiastic and active attendance;

- the Scientific Committee for selecting papers and organising the conference programme;

- all who supported the conference (sponsors, partners and volunteers) and particularly those who contributed to these Proceedings;

- the efsli team and the local Organising Committee for the excellent organisation of the efsli conference in Toulouse. Their dedication, support, advice, and motivation contributed to make the conference successful.

Ivana Bućko
efsli President

A multi-disciplinary approach to interpreting – improving communication by training medical students

Paul Belmonte and Shaurna Dickson (Deaf Action)

paul.belmonte@deafaction.org

Shaurna.dickson@deafaction.org

Abstract:

One of the main barriers to communication for Deaf people in healthcare situations is the lack of awareness of medical staff. Doctors and other professionals may be unmindful of the specific needs of Deaf patients, the importance of using an interpreter and of the best ways to work with a communication professional. Here, we present our innovative work in partnership with the University of Dundee to provide two weeks of bespoke training on their medical programme. As well as explaining the context in which we set up the training, we describe the content of the course and our approach to creating a dialogue with future medical professionals. Each time we have presented this course, we have found there to be a collaborative space in which all of us as Deaf people, communication professionals and future doctors have shared ideas and learned from each other's experience and approach. We then go on to describe the outcomes of the training that was provided and how the outlooks of all the participants were changed as a result. It is our hope that this presentation will provide a model from which other institutions might create similar programmes which would lead to an improved experience for Deaf patients using healthcare services.

Keywords:

Training, medical, doctors, interpreters, multi-disciplinary

1. Introduction

Health care should be accessible to everyone. However, for many Deaf people, barriers to effective medical treatment remain. According to the *Sick of It* report (Sign Health, 2014), in the UK, 70% of Deaf people who have not been to their GP recently wanted to, but did not go, mainly because there was no interpreter. Additionally, only 3% of Deaf people want to communicate with their doctor by lipreading, but 40% are forced to. Further, 8 in 10 Deaf people want to communicate using BSL, but only 3 in 10 are given the chance.

Certainly, within the UK, these barriers exist less because of a lack of interpreters and more due to a deficit in knowledge and awareness among medical professionals. For this reason, Deaf Action, a deaf-led organisation in Scotland, has been working with the University of Dundee to provide intensive deaf awareness training to medical students. This course is offered annually; in 2017, eleven students attended. The aim has been to equip doctors, right at the beginning of their career, with the knowledge and skills needed to improve the patient experience of deaf people, leading to better treatment outcomes. This training is unique in Scotland and similar programmes around the UK and Europe are rare.

2. Content

The course was offered as an elective module to students and classes were taught every day for two weeks. The programme taught skills in treating and communicating with patients with all types of deafness, including hard of hearing, deafened, signed language users and deafblind people. The timetable included:

- Deaf Awareness
- BSL (7 sessions)
- Audiology
- Equipment
- Deafness and Mental Health
- Lipreading, and
- How to work with an interpreter.

We recognise the importance of employing Deaf tutors to teach the course to the extent possible; classes in BSL and deafblind awareness were taught by Deaf people, using interpreters where necessary. One highlight of the module was the class taught by a Deaf mother with lived experience of accessing (and of struggling to access) health services. Hearing her first-hand accounts made an impact on the students present and helped them to think carefully about their future practice. As one student told us, "I feel you definitely learn more from a deaf person talking about their personal experiences than [from] someone else."

One day of the training was devoted to teaching students how to work with an interpreter. The class included open and dynamic discussions of:

- Why book an interpreter?
- What do interpreters do?
- What will interpreters not do?
- How will it affect my practice?
- Should I always book an interpreter?
- What would I do if the Deaf patient wanted to use a family member?
- Where to sit
- How to prepare

We then gave students the opportunity to consult with a Deaf person as their "patient", using the trainer as an interpreter. We were grateful to our Deaf participant who invented a long list of ailments to allow the students to practice their skills!

3. Outcomes

This session, along with the rest of the course, had positive outcomes for all involved. First of all, the presenter of the 'How to Work With an Interpreter' session was able to participate in cross-disciplinary discussion with a group of people who would soon be working as doctors. This led to a greater awareness of the needs and approach of clinicians and even to a change in practice.

Previously, the interpreter / trainer, in an effort to minimise his impact on interpreted interactions, had made it a practice not to introduce himself by name. More recent literature (Llewellyn-Jones and Lee, 2014) has stated that for an interpreter to fail to introduce themselves would cause damage to the communication event. The trainer was able to discuss this with the students; they agreed that for an interpreter to fail to give their name when introducing themselves would cause them to feel uncomfortable and inhibited in their communication. Since this discussion, the interpreter / trainer has modified his approach; an example of learning coming from cross-disciplinary discussions.

We have also learned about the process of taking a patient history from a doctor's perspective, as well as the amount of thought and training that goes into learning how to break bad news. This learning has been fed back to the interpreting team at Deaf Action and is also used as we teach student and trainee interpreters in the workplace.

These discussions between soon-to-be medical professionals and a language professional have created space for collaborative thinking, so our ways of working together can progress towards an agreed way of working that meets the needs of everyone involved (Ozolins, 2016).

There are also positive outcomes for Deaf patients. As students become qualified doctors, they will take their improved knowledge and working practices into their future careers and share them with their colleagues. This will lead to improved patient experiences for at least some deaf people (Hsieh et al., 2009). The fact that Deaf people were the primary deliverers of the training creates an ethos of co-production of services, leading to a sense of ownership and the creation of routes to further improvement. Acting as tutors also helps to empower Deaf people as individuals as they use their experience to influence service development and even to complain when their own care falls short.

For the students themselves, their interest in deaf issues was ignited, leading to increased knowledge and improved practice, which can be shared with future colleagues. They offered feedback such as, "I loved learning BSL" and "BSL classes were incredible". For eleven future doctors (from 2017 alone) to have this level of enthusiasm for sign language will surely make a difference to their attitudes and practice. Another student told us,

"I think every medical student should do this course. ... actually meeting Deaf BSL tutors [and] the interpreters and working with them ... has been an amazing experience and would be hugely beneficial to any medical student."

4. Next steps

Having delivered this module for a number of years, Deaf Action is continuing to look at ways to expand its reach. We are exploring the possibility of more cross-disciplinary training in breaking bad news, where student doctors and interpreters can learn together and improve their skills in this sensitive area. We were pleased to announce at the efsli conference that our two-week module has been expanded to fill four weeks of teaching, with extra time given to providing an accredited BSL qualification. We are also offering the module to other medical schools, with the aim of expanding good practice still further.

From the outcomes described, it is clear that this kind of multi-disciplinary working between interpreters, the medical profession and Deaf people has many positive outcomes. It is to be hoped that awareness and good practice spreads among medical professionals and that the barriers to health care described at the outset will lessen and eventually disappear.

Finally, this model of training need not be limited to clinicians. As language professionals, it is well worth considering who else we can work with and learn alongside. A multi-disciplinary approach brings many benefits and the success of this model can surely be replicated in other settings.

5. References

Hsieh, E., Ju, H, and Kong, H., 2010. Dimensions of trust: The tensions and challenges in provider-interpreter trust, *Qualitative Health Research* vol. 20, issue 2 pp.170-181

Llewellyn-Jones, P. and Lee, R., 2014 *Redefining the role of the community interpreter: The concept of role-space.* Lincoln, SLI Press

Ozolins, U., 2016. The myth of the myth of invisibility? *Interpreting* vol. 18 issue 2, pp. 273-284. Amsterdam, John Benjamins

Sign Health, 2014. *Sick of it – How the Health Service is failing Deaf people* available on-line http://www.signhealth.org.uk/health-information/sick-of-it-report/sick-of-it-in-english/

Contributors to this presentation:

Paul Belmonte is Senior Interpreter at Deaf Action in Scotland and has been interpreting for 12 years in a range of settings. He has delivered a number of conference workshops and is currently acting as a mentor for students and trainee interpreters.

Shaurna Dickson has been working as an interpreter for 16 years and is now the Communication and Training Manager at Deaf Action. She has worked in a wide range of interpreting domains and is also an experienced trainer.

The internal representations used by Sign Language Interpreters in the healthcare settings: description and didactic activities

Dr. Rayco H. González Montesino (Universidad Rey Juan Carlos, Madrid – Spain)

raycoh.gonzalez@urjc.es

Abstract:

In the training of Sign Language Interpreters, I am often faced with serious difficulties in making students understand the settings in which they will be involved in the future. Although we already have theoretical models on the process of interpretation (e.g. Cokely, 1992; Wilcox and Shaffer, 2005; Llewellyn-Jones and Lee, 2013), I consider it to be vital that future interpreters understand this process in the same way as any act of communication, with specific characteristics because it is a triadic situation, but that can be described by the general model of human communication.

To describe healthcare settings, or any others, and to design didactic activities to improve the proficiency of the students, I use the human communication model of Escandell Vidal (2005), based on Relevance Theory (Sperber and Wilson, 1986). This model is composed of: 1) elements, which are the physical components of the communicative act that can be directly observed (participants and signals, whether linguistic or not); 2) representations, or mental entities that have some type of function in the communicative event; and 3) processes, which correspond to the different types of operations that are put in place for communication to occur.

This paper aims to present a description of healthcare settings from a communicative and pragmatic perspective, using the internal representations that —in my view— any Sign Language Interpreters in our sociocultural environment would activate in these settings: communicative aim, setting, social distance, modes and the general and linguistic knowledge that facilitates their work. In addition, I will propose some didactic activities that allow the students to acquire such representations in their training process.

Keywords:

Sign language interpreting, healthcare settings, communication process, internal representations, didactic activities.

1. Introduction

The main aim of this work is to present a description of Sign Language Interpreting from a communicative and pragmatic perspective, in particular, that which is performed in medical settings.

In recent years, during my work as a Sign Language Interpreter Trainer, I have often found it difficult to help students acquire a holistic view about the act of interpretation, a vision which understands this linguistic and cultural intermediation as a communicative act which possesses specific features but, in the end, is an act in which two (or more than two) people try to exchange certain thoughts, ideas, beliefs, emotions and so on. In my PhD research, I studied sign language interpreting strategies but also, following Escandell Vidal's human communication model (2005), I described the five principal interpretation fields:

legal - administrative, religious, educational, conference and medical.

The latter is the field that I will briefly describe in this paper. To do this, I am going to highlight the internal mental representations that Sign Language Interpreters should possess and that they have to activate when they work in this domain. I am going to include a set of didactic activities too which help students to achieve this understanding of interpretation as a communicative and pragmatic act.

2. Sign Language Interpretation as an interlinguistic, intercultural and intermodal act of communication.

I understand Sign Language Interpreting as the tool through which two, or more than two, people with different languages and cultures deriving from a different hearing ability, can achieve full communication. It is an exceptional communicative act in which at least three main actors take part. One of them is the responsible for the inter-linguistic and intercultural mediation: The Sign Language Interpreter. This mediation is different from other inter-linguistic translation processes because of its intermodal character: it is performed from an auditory-oral language to a visual-gestural one. Therefore, the Sign Language Interpreter is a bilingual-bimodal interpreter, different from spoken languages interpreters, who can be considered as bilingual-unimodal interpreters (Nicodemus and Emmorey, 2013; Nicodemus, Swabey and Taylor, 2014).

Every act of communication is unique and unrepeatable, because it is produced by specific individuals, in a particular place and time under concrete circumstances. When a Sign Language Interpreter is also present, a new act of communication arises, a different and extraordinary one. The situation becomes more complex because the interpreter assumes a double function, in many cases at the same time: as the recipient of the original statement and as the speaker in the target language.

I agree with Escandell Vidal (2005) that the concept of human communication described in the classic model of Shannon and Weaver (1949, pp. 7-8) is mistaken and extremely simplistic. According to Relevance Theory (Sperber and Wilson, 1986), she proposes a new model of communication, that in my opinion, represents a more dynamic approach to this process. Communication implies that "[…] one (or several) individual (individuals) tries (try) to generate determined representations in another individual´s (people) mind." (Escandell Vidal, 2005, p. 40)[1].

This model is formed by:

1) elements, the physical components which can be directly observed: the speaker, the addressee and the linguistic or non-linguistic signals;

2) representations, or mental entities that possess any kind of function in the communicative event; and

3) processes, the different type of operations that occur: coding/decoding and manifestation/inference.

This new approach of human communication implies that a speaker with a communicative intention, keeping in mind the group of mental representations available to him, selects the signal best adapted to reach his objective. That signal, which can include linguistic or other type of elements, is subject to the decoding and inference process by the addressee through which he will create

---

[1] "[…] uno (o varios) individuo(s) trata(n) de originar determinadas representaciones en la mente de otro(s)" (Escandell Vidal, 2005, p. 40).

a new group of representations in his mind, similar (but not necessary identical) to the one the speaker wanted to transmit to him (ibid., p. 40)².

Because I want to outline my description of the medical field based upon the internal mental representations Sign Language Interpreters should have and employ at the time they are undertaking their task, I am going to explain these representations in more detail.

The Representations

In any kind of communicative act other essential factors intervene: situation, extra-linguistic reality, knowledge of the world and knowledge about interlocutor, etc. These very heterogeneous elements are included in what Escandell Vidal (2005) has denominated 'internal representations'. They are conceived of

> *[...] groups of propositions which detail the way in which we conceptualize the world around us, individuals and the relationship with them, and also our own intentions, desires and beliefs...* (ibid., p. 32).

The internal representations are individual and that is why they admit a high degree of complexity and details, while external representations, that is words or signs, are collectively used; consequently, they cannot reflect the singularities of each person. Linguistic expressions are "[...] simply effective and useful outlines which enable us to transmit something sufficiently

---

² "[...] como conjuntos de proposiciones que detallan el modo en el que conceptualizamos el mundo que nos rodea, los individuos y la relación que tenemos con ellos, y nuestras propias intenciones, deseos y creencias..." (Escandell Vidal, 2005, p. 32).

similar" (ibid., p. 33)³. This idea allows us to realize the great difficulty for the Sign Language Interpreter to achieve transmission of the speaker's internal representations to the addressee. By combining the processes of decoding and inference, the interpreter can only approach what the speaker is trying to transmit. However, he will never reach the goal of transmitting the actual internal representation.

Escandell Vidal (2005) presents the communicative context from a broader perspective, as a flexible group of representations typical of an individual and those he acquires in a physical or social environment. There are different elements in these representations which directly influence the production of language: the objective, the setting, the social distance and the mode.

3. Medical context and Signed Interpretation: a description according to shared representations.

I think medical interpreting is one of the most delicate interpretation fields because of the significance of the Sign Language Interpreter in the lives of the people involved.

As a general rule, the Spanish public health service does not take responsibility for the recruitment of staff Sign Language Interpreters. Interpreters usually work within associations for deaf people. These Sign Language Interpreters are not usually experts in health services, and they depend instead on their own knowledge and experience.

Sign Language Interpreter internal representations in the medical field

---

[3] "[…] simplemente esbozos eficaces y útiles que nos permiten transmitir algo suficientemente parecido" (Escandell Vidal, 2005, p. 33).

- **Communicative aim**

Interpreters can affirm that the communicative aim of a deaf user in this field is to transmit and receive information related to some aspect relating to his own health, or that of a relative.

As in any other field, the specific situation will also determine the real communicative aim. However, it is crucial that the Sign Language Interpreter has an internal representation of this objective. The closer the internal representation is to the reality, the better. It is therefore essential that the Sign Language Interpreter has all of the relevant information available about where he is going to work, which kind of medical service he is going to interpret, and who the participants are going to be (see De los Santos Rodríguez and Lara Burgos, 2004, p. 153).

- **Setting**

Medical interpretation services are as varied as they are unpredictable. This diversity is due to the personal characteristics and linguistic competences of the participants, but also to the topic and the place where it is carried out.

Sign Language Interpreters can be required for a multitude of situations. Nevertheless, it is fundamental that Sign Language Interpreters possess a mental outline of a medical appointment which allows them to anticipate problems and to better develop their work, specifying the resources and strategies to use. According to Byrne and Long (1976, cited in Angelelli, 2004, p. 75), any medical consultation is composed of six phases:

1. The relationship between doctor and patient is established.
2. The doctor tries to find out the reason for the patient's visit.

3. The doctor examines the patient physically or verbally, or both.
4. The doctor makes observations about the state of the patient.
5. Detailed explanation of the treatment or future tests required.
6. Consultation finishes, normally instigated by the doctor.

However, as Metzger (1999) points out, these stages have not to occur in isolation. Moreover, overlapping of the phases can occur, which may cause problems of interaction (see Metzger 1999, pp. 70-71). I agree with Angelelli (2004) that the simple presence of an interpreter influences the normal development of these six phases. In this way, in the first stage, when the relationship between doctor and patient is established, doctors usually confuse the role of the Sign Language Interpreter thinking he is a relative of the deaf person (Metzger 1999). It is recommended that the Sign Language Interpreter introduces himself and briefly explains his task when he enters.

It is also important to have an image of the place of interaction beforehand. As a general rule, medical consultations take place in a room, where there are usually two chairs where the deaf patient and the Sign Language Interpreter are invited to sit, although this is not the optimum place for the interpreter to undertake his task.

The positioning of the Sign Language Interpreter is extremely important. Generally, he should place himself sitting next to the doctor so that both professionals are in the deaf patient's visual field. Nevertheless, the arrangement of the furniture, or the lack of experience of the doctor in allowing this invasion of his workspace, can result in a triangle arrangement being the best option. In the phase when there are physical examinations and routine processes, the interpreter has to consider his location, because being next to the medical specialist could make the doctor's work difficult. In many cases, the presence of the Sign Language Interpreter can be embarrassing for the deaf person, especially in a physical exam. According to Napier, McKee and Goswell (2010, p. 119), to preserve patient privacy, a Sign Language Interpreter has to negotiate his positioning and use strategies to allow communication between the doctor and the patient.

Hearing participants may use the jargon of medical-health specialists, which has peculiarities that make communication very difficult and the task of the Sign Language Interpreter complex. The interpreter´s preparation of their service and specialization in the medical interpreting field is fundamental. The limited knowledge of deaf people of medical vocabulary, because of the lack of opportunities to access to it through signed languages, is also a problem because it not only prevents them from recognizing and understanding this jargon, but also from expressing what is happening with their health.

Regarding the linguistic choices of the interlocutors, we have to take into account the difference of linguistic modality between oral and sign languages. The doctor usually uses technical terms which have no direct equivalents in Sign Language. Although in recent years specific lexicographic material has been created in this field (Fundación CNSE, 2002), Sign Language Interpreters have to be cautious about its use, because deaf users usually do not consult this kind of bibliographic resource. They have also to take care with the excessive use of dactylology (fingerspelling) because deaf people usually do not know those technical terms and therefore they may not understand the information which is being transmitted to them (Moore and Swabey, 2007).

In the phase when the reasons for the consultation are given, the deaf patient usually uses very descriptive language, using space, iconicity, classifiers, etc. This means that the Sign Language

Interpreter has to find technical equivalents in the oral language, because this could be the expectation of the health professional.

In medical-health situations, there is usually not a high degree of control in terms of preparation of the Deaf patient's and doctor's statements, either beforehand or during the explanation. Normally, they are not based on written texts, which would allow organization of statements later on, and thus influence the choice of specific terms and structures used. Therefore, the Sign Language Interpreter is completely unaware of the kind of terms that are going to be used, and there could be statements with false beginnings and many hesitations from the deaf patient, because of his lack of knowledge about the topic.

The level of institutionalization in this kind of situation is relatively low, although it depends on the exact place of interpretation: there is a difference between an interaction between a primary health doctor and a deaf person, and a consultation with a forensic doctor as an 'expert witness' in court. It is true that formulaic greetings and other such fixed structures are usually used at certain times and some terms are not used, such as offensive language. Metzger (1999, pp. 69-74) found linguistic evidence which indicates that all participants in a real interpreted medical situation share a similar outline of certain stages that the situation will involve. Thus, the medical situation itself and the context where it takes place influence the linguistic choices of the participants, both deaf and hearing.

Moreover, there are differences between deaf people and health professionals regarding the schema they have of a situation interpreted by a Sign Language Interpreter, which directly influences the terms they use in their statements. According to Metzger (1999, p. 74), Doctors and health staff have not acquired this schema, and they use imperatives and the third person to refer to the deaf person. These linguistic elements evince that, in their internal representation of the situation of interpretation, they do not directly communicate with the deaf patient but indirectly through the Sign Language Interpreter. On the other hand, both deaf users and Sign Language Interpreters, through the use of the first person, evince that they understand the communication between the interlocutors in a direct way, without including the Sign Language Interpreter as a participant (see Metzger, 1999, p. 77).

Cultural differences and the expectations of each participant related to the linguistic choice of the other person are other issues to keep in mind in medical situations. Mindess (2006, pp. 158-160) comments on a series of examples of cultural discrepancies which usually take place in medical consultations with deaf patients, such as the detailed explanation of their medical history after the doctor says "Hello, how are you?".

Finally, the register used in this kind of communicative situation is also 'casual', slightly formal. However, I think the register used by deaf people is much more informal than would be expected of a hearing patient in this situation. The Sign Language Interpreter has to take into account all the variables in the meeting, and to adapt accordingly the register of his interpretation.

- **Social distance**

The difference in relative power between the interlocutors influences the choice of linguistic elements within their statements, as well as the control they have within the communicative situation. The image of Doctors and health staff in our society is one of a figure possessing a certain authority; this image is shared by deaf users, but also by Sign Language Interpreters themselves. So, they will face unequal communicative situations where health staff assume responsibility for the conversation, imposing the time allowed for speaking, the topic, etc.

It also needs to be remembered that the mental representations of healthcare staff are important, in relation to the social distance between them and the deaf patient - and even the Sign Language Interpreter himself, because it will determine their linguistic choices. If Doctors address their patients in an indirect way, we can assume that when they choose vocabulary and statements, they do not consider the deaf person, but rather the Sign Language Interpreter as the recipient of the utterance.

However, linguistic choices are also directly influenced by the degree of familiarity and empathy that the interlocutors have. I think that close contact over time between a health professional and a deaf person would create links, enabling a different representation of the Deaf person for the healthcare professional. This way, the language choices used in treatment by a medical professional gradually approach a more equal level.

Healthcare staff working in the area of hearing disability may also show more closeness and empathy with deaf people, because they are used to dealing with deaf people and they have specific training in this. Moreover, depending on the views they hold on deafness itself and deaf people, the Sign Language Interpreter will come across quite different terms being used. These linguistic choices allow the Sign Language Interpreter to know what the professional's position is regarding deaf people, their culture and language, and they can anticipate a lack of empathy and linguistic distance from the deaf interlocutor in their statements.

- **Modes**

The mode of communication generally used in medical situations is the oral mode, although written texts are also relevant, in the form of medical histories, diagnoses and treatments, admission and discharge reports, etc., which are recorded through this modality. The Sign Language Interpreter has to keep in mind the influence of this modality on the statements of the interlocutors. It should be pointed out that images and graphics appear in the results of tests such as radiography, scans, audiometry, etc. In these cases, the Sign Language Interpreter has to use the spatial and visual-gestural resources of Sign Languages to represent this information in a three-dimensional way, and also must possess a wide knowledge of the tests and their procedures.

Many times, mostly in emergency situations, and when there is a difficulty in communicating through oral or visual-gestural means, the interlocutors use writing as a communication method. This can be misleading because of the difference in the syntactic structure between written language and Sign Language (see Meador and Zazove, 2005, p. 219). For this reason, it is important that health professionals and the institutions responsible for providing this kind of services be aware of the diversity of communication methods used by deaf people, and about the difficulties some of them could have in terms of receiving appropriate medical attention. They should also be aware of the need to determine the communication preferences of deaf patients (Moore and Swabey, 2007; Polanco Teijo and García-Ruise, 2010; Chaveiro, Porto and Barbosa, 2009; Iezzoni *et al.*, 2004.).

- **General and linguistic knowledge**

It is necessary that Sign Language Interpreters know the fundamental aspects of the different medical specializations, the main diseases and clinical procedures, etc. The diversity of medical and health specializations means that the terminology used is very wide and varied, with many homonymous terms, the meaning of which is difficult to access without previous training.

As De los Santos Rodríguez and Lara Burgos (2004, p. 154) affirm, a Sign Language Interpreter must possess good general knowledge and know where the different organs are located in the body, because in Spanish Sign Language most of these signs are deictics (ibid., pp. 156-157). Knowledge related to the sense of hearing has particular relevance: the anatomy and physiology of the ear, medical and health specializations directly or indirectly connected to hearing impairment, technical aids, and the diagnostic tests that are normally used and the way they are carried out. He also has to be informed about the latest technological and procedural developments in this field, because progress in this is constant, and such knowledge can quickly become outdated.

On the other hand, a Sign Language Interpreter has to be aware of the internal representations among deaf people of the healthcare system and healthcare professionals. Polanco Teijo and García-Ruise (2010) affirm that, due to the experiences they have had, many deaf people feel that difficulties, communication barriers and lack of access to information are bigger issues for them in healthcare settings than in other fields. These problems of communication cause feelings of fear, mistrust and frustration in deaf patients (Chaveiro, Porto and Barbosa, 2009, p. 148). Many of them think that certain health professionals do not see them as independent and self-reliant individuals, and they do not respect them.

The Sign Language Interpreter also has to be aware of the internal representations among health staff of deaf patients, and to understand the fear they feel when communicating with deaf patients for the first time, due to lack of awareness and specific training. It is therefore a priority to provide specific training to healthcare staff in order that they achieve an understanding of the behaviors, cultural values and opinions of deaf people (see Mindess, 2006, pp. 159-160).

4. A proposal of didactic activities

Finally, I would like to mention some ideas for work in the classroom with students about these internal representations, with the aim of acquiring and employing them.

Beyond working in this field with medical texts, and teaching them specific vocabulary in sign language, I consider that the first thing is to discuss how the communicative process between people works, and how the presence of the Sign Language Interpreter influences the normal communicative act. This should be complemented by visualizing the scenario, for example, using some of the different videos that can be found on the internet, where one can see how a medical consultation proceeds, the use of language by medical specialists, the layout of furniture in the rooms, etc. These videos, once a discursive analysis has been carried out, will be interpreted by the students in the classroom, who will consider the problems that arise and what strategies to use to solve them. It is also essential to carry out role-playing activities in which different situations in health settings are simulated.

In order to observe how a deaf patient and a doctor interact, it would be recommended that students accompany professional interpreters, and observe how the medical situation proceeds and how the professional interpreter solves various problems.

5. Conclusions

In conclusion, I agree with Llewellyn-Jones and Lee (2013) when they affirm that it is fundamental to know how two people who do not need a mediator communicate, in order to better understand our work and to develop an effective interpretation. I believe that it is necessary for future Sign Language Interpreters to acquire, during their training, a vision of interpretation as a communicative and pragmatic act, in which we must try to get as close as possible to the internal representations of the speaker/signer, and to transmit these through whatever external representations that the target language allows us, with the aim of generating within the addressee corresponding internal representations.

I share with Roy (2000), Leeson (2005) and Wilcox and Shaffer (2005) the opinion that the Sign Language Interpreter is an active participant in the interpretation situation and that the success or failure of it depends, in many cases, on the decisions of the interpreter. It is essential that interpreting students are aware of this and not only acquire the internal representations which I have outlined today, but also employ them within different health settings.

6. References

Angelelli, C. V. (2004) *Medical interpreting and cross-cultural communication*. Cambridge: Cambridge University Press.

Chaveiro, N., Porto, C. C., & Barbosa, M. A. (2009) The Relation Between Deaf Patients and the Doctor. *Brazilian Journal of Otorhinolaryngology*, **75**(1), pp.147-150. [Accessed 17 Dec. 2017].

Available at:
http://www.scielo.br/pdf/rboto/v75n1/en_v75n1a23.pdf

Cokely, D. (1992) *Sign language Interpreters and Interpreting*. Burtonsville, MD: Linstok Press.

De los Santos Rodríguez, E. & Lara Burgos, M. P. (2004) *Técnicas de interpretación de lengua de signos.* 2nd ed. Madrid: Fundación CNSE.

Escandell Vidal, M. V. (2005) *La comunicación*. Madrid: Editorial Gredos S.A.

Fundación CNSE (2002) *Glosarios en lengua de signos española*. Madrid: Fundación CNSE para la Supresión de las Barreras de Comunicación.

Iezzoni, L. I., O'Day, B. L., Killeen., M., & Harker, H. (2004) Communicating about Health Care: Observations from Persons Who Are Deaf or Hard of Hearing. *Annals of Internal Medicine*, **140**(5), pp.356-362. [Accessed 20 Dec. 2017]. Available at: <http://dredf.org/healthcare-stories/wp-content/uploads/sites/2/2012/05/DEAF-and-HH-Communicating-About-Health-Care1.pdf>.

Leeson, L. (2005) Making the effort in simultaneous interpreting. Some considerations for signed language interpreters. In T. Janzen (Ed.), *Topics in Signed Language Interpreting*. Amsterdam/Philadelphia: John Benjamins B.V.

Llewellyn-Jones, P., & Lee, R. G. (2013) Getting to the Core of Role: Defining Interpreters' Role-Space. *International Journal of Interpreter Education*, **5**(2), pp.54-72.

Meador, H., & Zazove, P. (2005). Health Care Interactions with Deaf Culture. *Journal of the American Board of Family Medicine*, **18**(3), pp.218-222. DOI: http://dx.doi.org/10.3122/jabfm.18.3.218

Metzger, M. (1999) *Sign language interpreting: Deconstructing the myth of neutrality*. Washington, D.C: Gallaudet University Press.

Mindess, A. (2006) *Reading between the signs. Intercultural communication for sign language interpreters*. 2nd ed. Yarmouth, MN: Intercultural Press

Moore, J., & Swabey, L. (2007) *Medical Interpreting: A Review of the Literature*. Catie: College of St. Catherine/NCIEC

Napier, J., McKee, R. L., & Goswell, D. (2010) *Sign language interpreting: Theory and practice in Australia and New Zealand*. Annandale, N.S.W: Federation Press.

Nicodemus, B., & Emmorey, K. (2013) Direction asymmetries in spoken and signed language interpreting. *Bilingualism: Language and Cognition*, **16**(3), pp.624-636. DOI: http://dx.doi.org/10.1017/S1366728912000521

Nicodemus, B., Swabey, L., & Taylor, M. M. (2014) Preparation strategies used by American Sign Language-English interpreters to render President Barack Obama's inaugural address. *The Interpreters' Newsletter*, 19, pp.27-44. [Accessed 21 Dec. 2017]. Available at: http://hdl.handle.net/10077/10648

Polanco Teijo, F., & García-Ruise, S. (2010) Necesidad sentida de las mujeres sordas durante el parto y el puerperio inmediato en el ámbito hospitalario. In: *Cultura de los cuidados, 28*, pp.49-56. [Accessed 18 Dec. 2017]. Available at: http://rua.ua.es/dspace/bitstream/10045/16331/1/CC_28_07.pdf

Roy, C. B. (2000) *Interpreting as a discourse process*. New York: Oxford University Press.

Sperber, D., & Wilson, D. (1986/1994) *La relevancia. Comunicación y procesos cognitivos*. Madrid: Visor.

Shannon, C. E., & Weaver, W. (1949) *The mathematical theory of communication*. Urbana: The University of Illinois Press.

Wilcox, S., & Shaffer, B. (2005) Towards a cognitive model of interpreting. In T. Janzen (Ed.), *Topics in Signed Language Interpreting*. Amsterdam/Philadelphia: John Benjamins B.V.

Contributor to this presentation:

Dr. Rayco H. González Montesino Graduated in Speech Therapy from the University of La Laguna and in Social and Cultural Anthropology from the Universidad Nacional de Educación a Distancia (UNED), he is a Doctor Cum Laude in Applied Linguistics from the University of Vigo with the thesis *La estrategia siempre a mano: propuestas didácticas para la interpretación en lengua de signos*, the first in Spain to take the sign language interpreting as an object of study and analysis. In addition, he completed the Master's Degree in Inclusive Education and the Master's Degree in Interpretation of Spanish Sign Language, both organized by the University of La Laguna. Since 2002 he has worked as a sign language interpreter in different settings, although mainly in the higher education field. At the same time, he has worked since 2004 as trainer of sign language interpreters in the official interpreter training program in Spain. This academic year 2017-2018 he is a university professor and researcher on the only degree program that currently trains interpreters in Spain: Degree of Spanish Sign Language and Deaf Community of the University Rey Juan Carlos, Madrid. His main areas of interest and research are sign language interpretation and translation, didactic training of interpreters, learning sign language as a L2 and the Deaf Community.

# The use of Situated Learning in the training of Sign Language Interpreters working in Healthcare domains.

Thaïsa Hughes and Sarah Bown (University of Wolverhampton)

thaisa.hughes@wlv.ac.uk,

s.bown@wlv.ac.uk

Abstract:

Sign Language interpreters can be asked to work across the whole of the healthcare sector, within a range of appointments. Therefore, it is incumbent upon interpreter educators to provide training opportunities which adequately prepare student interpreters for work in these assignments. The University of Wolverhampton has used the concept of 'Situated Learning' (Lave and Wenger, 1991) to create educational experiences that mimic, so far as is feasible, the type of healthcare scenarios that student interpreters are likely to come across most regularly.

Keywords:

Situated learning; healthcare interpreting; medical interpreting.

1. Introduction

Student interpreters need to be prepared for the linguistic and cultural elements of their role, the variety of professionals they may encounter in the work place, and the protocols inherent within a multitude of settings. Interpreters who work in healthcare settings bear witness to some of the most sensitive and private appointments in a deaf person's life. The notion that Sign language Interpreting is a Practice profession (Dean and Pollard, 2013) brings up interesting questions for interpreter training, in terms of understanding the pedagogical methods that other practice professions use in training their future professionals.

One of the inherent difficulties in delivering healthcare training is the fact that often experiences have to be simulated via in-class roleplays.

With this in mind, we have looked at the profession of Nursing (a well-established practice profession) and their use of 'situated learning/situated cognition' (Hung and Der- Thanq 2001) and high-fidelity simulation (Richardson and Claman, 2014) to train medical students.

In the academic year 2015/16, a pilot was undertaken at the University of Wolverhampton to train final-year undergraduate sign language interpreting students in healthcare interpreting, in the simulation suite which is used to train undergraduate nursing students. This suite is a state-of-the-art mock clinical environment, complete with hospital wards and mannequins that react appropriately to medical intervention.

The training was delivered by two Senior Lecturers, who are also registered qualified British Sign Language (BSL)/English interpreters, and a Senior Lecturer in nursing who is a registered adult health nurse. Following this pilot, a questionnaire and interviews were undertaken to determine whether the experience was useful and how it could be improved upon for future cohorts.

Following that feedback, the session was run again in 2016/17, with the addition of a Deaf BSL using participant, who took the part of the patient in a series of roleplays and subsequent discussions and review.

In traditional in-class roleplays, the roles of deaf/hearing consumers are often played by tutors and students. Whilst this approach is used successfully as a strategy in initial training, it does have some limitations. As Wadensjö (2014) highlights, issues can arise during these roleplay scenarios when the participants in a roleplay also have other relationships (i.e. those of tutor and student). It can be difficult not to switch between the role of tutor/student and the roleplay characters, breaking out of the character assigned and therefore making the interaction less realistic.

Student interpreters may be relatively relaxed when interpreting a role play in a classroom situation, as they know that a tutor playing the part of a deaf participant or a hearing person does in fact understand both languages and is therefore not actually reliant upon the interpretation provided by them.

The switching of frame between roleplay character and tutor/student described above, is less likely to happen if the participants in the roleplay are not regular tutors and if the situation in which the roleplay takes place is less like the classroom environment, as the classroom can "involve knowledge that is abstract, unconnected and decontextualized" (González-Davies and Enríquez-Raído, 2016).

As a result, interpreter educators must explore opportunities to give students an authentic experience, where participants are genuinely reliant upon the students' interpretation to communicate effectively with one another. Then the student may experience something that is as close to a real-life situation as possible, in order to prepare them effectively.

Our presentation at the efsli '2017 'What's up Doc?' conference, detailed the steps taken by lecturers at the University of Wolverhampton to find innovative ways to provide appropriately engaging and realistic simulated healthcare interpreting assignment experiences for the final year BSL/English interpreting cohort by using 'situated -earning'.

2. Methodology

In recent years, sign language interpreting has started to be viewed as a "practice profession in contrast to being a technical profession". (Dean and Pollard 2013, p. XIII) "...where complex, social context judgments and skills are crucial supplements to one's technical abilities". (Dean and Pollard 2009, p.1)

This idea of interpreting as a practice profession led us to explore the pedagogical methods employed by other such practice professions, most notably, Nursing, who employ High-Fidelity Simulation (HFS) techniques in their HE training programmes, via the use of simulation suites and technological aids which offer nursing students the opportunity to undertake clinical procedures on high-tech mannequins, in a mock hospital environment before doing so on a live patient.

The use of HFS within the situated cognition framework relocates learning from the decontextualized traditional teaching paradigm to a real-world human activity paradigm (Paige and Daley, 2009, p.102). *"...situated cognition implies that the activities of person and environment are parts of a mutually constructed whole"* (Hung and Der-Thanq 2001, p.8). This relocation of teaching and learning used in the training of healthcare workers, is also possible for interpreting students.

According to Richardson and Claman, HFS offers students "a nonthreatening environment, enhanced learning, and the feeling of being prepared to practice" (2014, p.127). This is obviously something that can benefit student interpreters.

The term 'situated-learning' was first coined by Lave and Wenger (1991), who discuss the fact that, learners inevitably participate in communities of practitioners and that the "mastery of knowledge and skill requires newcomers to move toward full participation in the socio-cultural practices of a community" (1991, p.29). The idea being that new members of the community (in this case of sign language interpreters) interact with 'old timers' in the domain relevant to that particular community in order to begin their journey to membership and later full participation. Lave and Wenger, for their exploration, studied apprenticeship amongst several different communities of practice, including: Midwives, Military Quartermasters, Butchers and Non-drinking alcoholics.

The use of both situated-learning and HFS, offers sign language interpreting students the opportunity to develop their community of practice within a training environment, with professionals from other disciplines. They are therefore able, given this new perspective, to also consider the communication aims of those participants and their inherent protocols/ code of ethics or conduct when undertaking an assignment.

Most BSL/English interpreters will regularly work in clinical/health-related environments, where there is a duty to ensure that deaf people "can communicate effectively with health and social care services" (NHS 2016). It was therefore decided that students would benefit from undertaking roleplay scenarios situated in a clinical environment, where they would interpret for a real healthcare practitioner and (in the second iteration of the training) a deaf person taking the role of the patient. These roleplays formed part of a series of activities linked to the topic of medical/healthcare interpreting.

The University of Wolverhampton has a state-of-the-art clinical simulation suite which is used to train Nurses and Healthcare professionals. We enlisted the support of a colleague from the Faculty of Health, Education and Wellbeing (FHEW), who is a Senior Lecturer in Adult Nursing. We designed a pilot session to trial the benefits of this type of situated-learning with our 2015/16 final year cohort who were undertaking a simultaneous interpreting module. Then, following feedback from all participants, we slightly amended the design of the session for delivery in 2016/17 and most recently to our 2017/18 cohort.

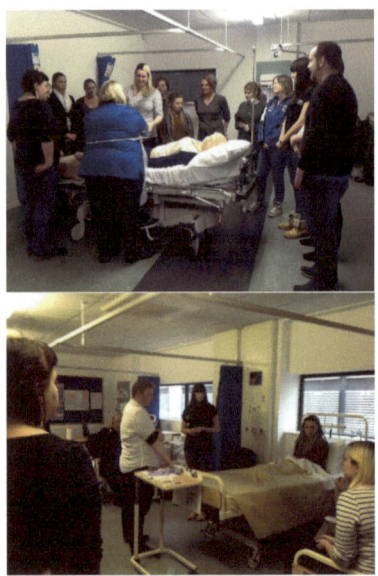

Fig 1 and Fig 2- Final year BSL/English Interpreting students being led through post-operative procedures by the nurse practitioner

In the initial sessions, the topic of medical interpreting was covered over a one-week period to ensure that learning was appropriately 'scaffolded' to help to create the internal coping structures for managing stress within practice, guide the thinking process, …suitable responses and inform appropriate decisions (Bown, 2013, p.55)

In order to maximise the time spent within the clinical skills lab, the students were set preparatory tasks to undertake, which included;

- Participating in an online lecture about interpreting in healthcare settings.

- Reading academic papers relating to interpreting in healthcare assignments, for example; Major and Napier (2012) and Schofield and Mapson (2014).

- Completing a situational analysis based upon photographs of medical environments/ scenarios (Davis, 2005).

- Interpreting video clips of deaf BSL users talking about their medical experiences.

Week 6	Monday am 31/10/16 (SB) 6IG002	Monday pm 31/10/16 (SB)	SDL	Tuesday am 6IG005 1/11/16 (TW)	Tuesday pm 1/11/16 (TW)	SDL
Clips	MH- Medical experiences	KM - Medical experiences	Situational analysis Dr's office.	Intro to the clinical skills lab table- allocation of roles etc.	Meet the heart interpretation task.	Diabetes info page Type 2 Diabetes
Pre-reading	Roy, C. B. (1992) A sociolinguistic analysis of the interpreter's role in simultaneous talk in a face-to-face interpreted dialogue. *Sign Language Studies*, 74, pp.21-61. Stone, C. (2010). Access all areas - sign language interpreting, is it that special? *Journal of Specialised Translation*, 14, pp.41-54. (http://www.jostrans.org/issue14/art_stone.php)		Situational analysis Hospital ward	NCIHC (2003) Guide to Interpreter positioning in Healthcare settings. *The National Council in Healthcare working paper series.* Major, G. and Napier, J. (2011) Interpreting and knowledge mediation in the healthcare setting: What do we really mean by "accuracy"? *Linguistica Antverpiensa*, 11, pp.207-225.	Online medical interpreting lecture. (See WOLF) Appendicitis information Gastroenteritis information	
Roleplay						
Situational analysis	Dr's office and hospital ward for SDL- using template.					

Fig 3 An example of the structure of the period leading up to the session in the clinical skills lab.

The BSL language teaching and interpreting curricula were aligned to ensure that students came to the clinical skills lab armed with appropriate healthcare-related vocabulary and an understanding of some of the demands they may face within medical assignments. They therefore arrived with a level of prepared ability or "prior knowledge" (Biggs 2000, p.13).

After consultation with the Nurse practitioner, a series of roleplays were constructed for use in the clinical skills lab that represented examples of some of the most common medical conditions that interpreters may regularly be interpreting. In the pilot in 2015/16, students played the parts of both deaf patients and interpreters and were given information about their roles one week in advance to allow them to undertake the necessary research.

Approximately two-weeks post session delivery, the 2015/16 cohort were asked to evaluate its efficacy via a questionnaire. Students were then asked if they were prepared to be interviewed. All of the students responded to the questionnaire and 2 agreed to be interviewed, one face-to-face and one by Skype.

The feedback received from the 2015/16 and subsequently the 2016/17 cohorts was used to tweak the programme for future delivery.

3. Findings

2015/16

The feedback from 2015/16 pilot was overwhelmingly positive. Students reported that the activities promoted a high level of engagement and motivation during the session. In response to a question about whether the same level of engagement could have been achieved in a classroom setting, 100% of the respondents replied no.

> *The classroom environment would not have allowed us to explore the importance of interpreter positioning in the way we did. Being in the medical wing gave me a chance to see just how close together patient beds are positioned, and the limited amount of space there*

> *is for an interpreter by the time you add in medical professional/s, equipment and family members into the space.* Student A

> *The day was really well planned, an amazing experience close to real life...* Student C

The level of engagement with the preparatory activities was exceptionally high too, with all of the students completing tasks such as the situational analysis (Davis, 2005, Kurz, 2001), the video and audio lectures and the video clips of deaf people using BSL to relay their medical experiences. 91.6% of students had also engaged with the recommended academic literature.

In a bid to further enhance the student experience we asked for activity-improvement feedback

Students felt that having the Nurse practitioner in the roleplays was so valuable because she did not know any sign language and was able to react purely based upon the interpretation provided. They felt that they would have liked to have had a deaf roleplay participant who was also fully reliant upon their interpretation, to add to the authenticity of the experience.

> *... the feeling of the setting and specific equipment along with the benefit of a medically qualified non-signing participant was specific to the environment.* Student D

As a result of the 2015/16 student feedback, when delivering the session to the 2016/17 and 2017/18 cohorts, we brought in a deaf BSL user to play the part of the patient in the roleplays and again used a hearing healthcare professional who did not know any sign language.

2016/17

The 2016/17 cohort were asked a series of questions prior to receiving the teaching related to healthcare interpreting and prior to the simulation suite event, to determine some of their thoughts around medical interpreting assignments.

At that point, 80% of the cohort felt that they were interested in undertaking medical interpreting assignments in the future.

80% of them had no previous healthcare interpreting experience.

When asked how difficult they anticipated healthcare interpreting would be (on a scale of 10), the average result was 6.7. The difficulties that they anticipated mainly centred around; being able to control their own emotions, understanding medical terminology and the physical positioning of the interpreter given that patients may be reclining, lying face down etc. during examinations.

Before the session took place, students were not confident that they understood what the domain of medical interpreting entailed- giving their level of confidence about this as 4.5/10.

An extended period of an extra week was given to the topic, which provided more time to cover some of the theoretical aspects outside of the simulation suite. We adjusted the programme to ensure that, as well as the hours of preparatory activities, the class lectures, the interpretations of videoed material, and the opportunity to observe their peers interpreting, each student had a minimum of 7.5 minutes interpreting on the day with the two participants, as well as time to debrief with the Nurse and deaf patient.

Using a framework of 'cognitive apprenticeship' (Collins, Brown and Holum, 1991) to look at the efficacy of the session design, we also included a chance for 'articulation' and 'reflection' to take place, whereby students were asked to review a video clip of the interpretation that they had done, and to undertake a written reflective analysis in order to get "students to articulate their knowledge, reasoning, or problem-solving processes" (Collins et al., 1991, p.14).

2016/17 cohort post session

When the revised two-week period spent focusing on healthcare interpreting had come to an end, a second questionnaire was administered to gather the views of the students about what they felt they had gained from the experience.

70% of students responded to the post event survey. 100% of those responding felt that the session had been a useful and enjoyable learning experience.

100% of respondents felt it was of equal importance to have all the experts (the qualified interpreter trainers, the healthcare professional and the deaf person) present on the day.

> *To enable students to get the most out of the experience and to make it as close to the situations we will soon find ourselves in, the presence of a Registered Adult Nurse and a Visiting Deaf Lecturer were paramount. Module tutors guided students through the day, giving advice and constructive feedback throughout.* Participant 3

The realistic nature of the encounter was remarked upon frequently by respondents:

> *... the real experience was fantastic.... I have done volunteering recently which has presented similar difficulties and left me feeling quite low, however being*

> *able to discuss issues and what went wrong turns a negative experience into a learning opportunity.* Participant 1
>
> *No matter how much we set up scenarios in class, nothing would have been as good and beneficial than being in a simulated environment such as the lab*
>
> *Researching topics in preparation for the role plays enabled me to realise that this is an area I enjoy and am interested in.* Participant 2

This student feedback reinforced the need for the students to undertake the preparatory activities in order to scaffold their learning and allow them to gain the maximum benefit from the day in the clinical skills lab.

85% of respondents felt that, based on their experiences of the healthcare interpreting preparation and session in the clinical skills lab, they were now more likely to be interested in undertaking medical interpreting assignments in the future. This demonstrates that the session raises aspirations and promotes skills which are likely to enhance employability, as well as providing greater access for the deaf community in the future by ensuring that the interpreters they will encounter in their medical appointments are suitably skilled and prepared.

All students stated that they did not feel that a session taking place in the classroom would have been as beneficial to their learning.

In addition to seeking feedback from the student interpreters, we also interviewed the healthcare professional and deaf participant. Their views are recounted below.

Nurse practitioner perspective

The whole theory behind learning in the skills lab is that it's a safe environment. Students can make mistakes; in simulation no one dies, there's no actual harm as a consequence of making errors, it's a safe place to practice, to self-reflect and to receive expert and peer feedback.

I feel there is equal value in learning for interpreters and healthcare professionals on how to work collaboratively to achieve the shared aim of helping the service user cope with their healthcare experience.

Deaf participant perspective

The activities undertaken in the clinical skills lab were based around some of the more common illnesses/conditions like; diabetes, blood pressure, a GP consultation, a physio appointment etc. Doing those kinds of common appointments now, helps the students envisage ways to cope when they encounter these same appointments in real life.

It provides an unbelievably valuable experience for the students and I have really enjoyed myself! I am delighted that this session has taken place and really hope there will be more sessions like this in the future. It really will help the students develop in readiness for their life as a working interpreter.

4. Conclusions

The use of situated-learning/ high-fidelity simulation to teach healthcare interpreting to final year BSL/English interpreting students was highly successful in engaging students, not only in the preparatory activities they were required to undertake, but also in the roleplays themselves and in the subsequent reflective analysis.

For anyone interested in undertaking this type of training, there were several key points which need to be considered.

- Preparatory activities- use a range of media to satisfy different cohort learning styles.

- Use external participants and professionals relevant to the employment domain- Link activities directly to employability/ world of work.

- Select roleplay themes based on those most likely to be experienced by students in the near future.

- Film roleplays where possible, to support the reflective activity which takes place post event.

- Phasing and structure (consider the pacing/ intensity of the session)

- Establish the idea of 'safe space' during the introduction/ welcome to the session to encourage students to feel confident to participate without fear of negative evaluation.

- Evaluate the session quite quickly, whilst it is still fresh in the students'/participants minds

- Utilise mixed media for gathering data

Whilst designing this type of situated-learning opportunity is reasonably time consuming in the initial stages, once the format is established, it is easy to run subsequent sessions using the same framework. In the BSL/English interpreting programme at the

University of Wolverhampton, these situated-learning principles have already now been applied to other interpreting domains, such as; interpreting for a home visit with a social worker, legal settings, sight translation and media translation and we look forward to exploring its use in other domains in the future.

Fig 4 Students working in the media studio

Fig 5 students engaged in roleplays in the social work flat

5. References

Biggs J. (2000) *Teaching for quality learning at university*. Buckingham: OUP & SRHE

Bown, S. (2013) Autopoiesis: scaffolding the reflective practitioner toward employability. In *International Journal of Interpreter Education* 5(1), pp.51-63.

Collins, A., Brown, J.S. & Holum, A. (1991) Cognitive Apprenticeship: Making thinking Visible. *American Educator, the quarterly journal of the American Federation of Teachers.*

Davis, J.E. (2005) Teaching Observation Techniques to Interpreters. In Roy, C. (ED) *Advances in Teaching Sign Language Interpreters*. Gallaudet University Press: Washington DC.

Dean, R, K. & Pollard, R, Q. (2009) *"I don't think we are supposed to be talking about this": Case conferencing and supervision for interpreters.* Retrieved from http://www.avlic.ca/sites/default/files/docs/AVLICNewsSF2013DeanPollardArticle.pdf

Dean, R. K. & Pollard, R. Q. (2013) *dc-s. The Demand Control schema: Interpreting as a Practice Profession.*

González-Davies. M. & Enríquez-Raído, V. (2016) Situated learning in translator and interpreter training: bridging research and good practice. *The Interpreter And TranslatorTrainer*.10(1),pp.1-11.Retrievedfrom http://www.tandfonline.com/doi/pdf/10.1080/1750399X.2016.1154339?needAccess=true (last accessed 21/3/2017).

Hung, D. & Der-Thanq, C. (2001) Situated Cognition, Vygotskian Thought and Learning from the Communities of Practice Perspective: Implications for the Design of Web-Based E-

Learning. *Education Media International.* 2(12) Retrieved from http://www.tandf.co.uk/journals

Kurz, I. (2001) Conference Interpreting: Quality in the Ears of the User. *Meta: journal des traducteurs / Meta: Translators' Journal*, 46(2), pp.394-409. Retrieved from http://www.erudit.org/revue/meta/2001/v46/n2/003364ar.pdf

Lave, J. & Wenger, E. 1991. *Situated Learning: Legitimate Peripheral Participation.* Cambridge: Cambridge University Press.

Major, G. & Napier, J. (2012) Interpreting and knowledge mediation in the healthcare setting: What do we really mean by "accuracy"? *Linguistica Antverpietsia- themes in Translation Studies.* (11) Retrieved from: https://lans-tts.uantwerpen.be/index.php/LANS-TTS/article/view/304/194

NHS (2016) *Accessible information standard.* Retrieved from https://www.england.nhs.uk/ourwork/accessibleinfo/

Onello, R. & Regan, M. (2013) Challenges in High Fidelity Simulation: Risk Sensitization and Outcome Measurement. *Online Journal of Issues in Nursing.* 18(3)

Paige, J, B. & Daley, B, J. (2009). Situated cognition: A learning framework to support and guide high fidelity simulation. In *Clinical simulation in Nursing.* 5, e97-e103. www.elsevier.com/locate/ecsn

Richardson, K, J. & Claman, F. (2014) High-Fidelity Simulation in Nursing Education: A Change in Clinical Practice. *Nursing Education perspectives.* 35(2), pp.125-127

Schofield, M. & Mapson, R. (2014) Dynamics in interpreted interactions: An insight into the perceptions of healthcare professionals. *Journal of Interpretation* 23(1), pp.1-15.

Wadensjö, C. (2014) Perspectives on role play: analysis, training and assessments, *The Interpreter and Translator Trainer*, 8(3), pp.437-451

Contributors to this presentation:

Thaïsa Hughes: is a part-time Senior Lecturer in Deaf studies and Interpreting and also works as a freelance registered sign language interpreter and assessor.

Sarah Bown: is a Senior Lecturer in Deaf studies and Interpreting and is a registered sign language interpreter with decades of experience in interpreting, educating and management.
s.bown@wlv.ac.uk

Sign Language in Worldwide Medicine

Dr Jean Dragon

jeandagron@yahoo.fr

Understanding and being understood by one's doctor: this seems a fundamental human right, even more so for someone in need of treatment, someone tired or anxious. It however remains out of reach for part of the population: the deaf. They, who think and dream in images, are confronted by health systems that ignore their linguistic and cultural *norms* or *background*. A deaf person's choice of language during consultation is not taken into account. The imposed language is written or oral. Thus, intolerable situations emerge.

An 8-year-old child has to announce that he has cancer to his parents, a deaf couple suffering from insulin-dependent diabetes and forgotten by a deficient health system. This happens everywhere around the globe. In Africa, a deaf woman explains by gestures that she is pregnant and suffers from intolerable pain. Thought to be a beggar, she is thrown out of the hospital.

These situations rightly outrage, but once the scandal fades, deaf people *return immediately to* invisibility. This lack of respect for the individual leads to late diagnosis and incorrect administration of the prescription by the deaf patient. The few existing studies show a silent minority lacking appropriate medical treatment and, in times of epidemics, left without information or, in some countries, without any access to treatment.

Yet sign language, cheaper than some sophisticated technologies, immediately makes treatment available. Of the 70 billion deaf people living worldwide, a few dozen thousands already benefit from it through interpreter services and/or specific medical spaces where nursing staff, deaf intermediaries and social workers communicate in sign language. In Europe, Central and South America, these new bonds create hope amongst the deaf community. Nursing staff can develop a visual thinking process to explain medical concepts. This visual-gestural communication could also benefit other patients.

Some treatments for meningitis or resilient forms of tuberculosis save lives but provoke secondary deafness. Sign language also attracts many newly deaf individuals who wish to defeat their social isolation.

No international framework specifically addresses deaf people's equality in medical care access. However, the International Convention on the Rights of Persons with Disabilities took a first legal step by stipulating that any confidentiality breach is discriminatory.

In France, HIV positive deaf people refused to consult doctors due to the obligation of doing so with a family member. This led to the opening of the pilot-consultation at the Salpêtrière in 1995.

Building on this legal argument of non-discrimination, which dozens of countries have now ratified, and on the records of sign language consultations already installed, **we ask that the choice be given for the use of sign language in a medical context worldwide.** It would *represent* social progress for millions of deaf people as well as a response to health emergencies in disaster affected countries.

(advocacy from Sources - mail : sourcesls20@gmail.com   site : sign-care.info

http://chn.ge/2G8XdBJ

Contributor to this presentation:

Dr Jean Dragon is a Doctor of Medicine, 1979 Diu phoniatrics 1991 DEA Social Psychology, 1993- School Advanced Studies in Social Sciences. He has been involved in the design and implementation of an access device for the care of deaf patients in France since 1992

He has participated in the creation of consultations in sign language as follows: Uruguay (2012). Tunisia (2016), Argentina (Health Fe 2016), Chile (Valparaiso 2017). Current projects: Cameroon, Colombia, Burkina Faso, Malaysia.

Book publications include;

1) "The silent. Chronicles of twenty years of medicine with the Deaf "Preface. Pr Sicard- Press Pluriel, Paris. 2008

2) "Palabras silenciosas" - Publishing crilence.2012

3) "Advocacy: access to treatments and care for Deaf People" - Publishing crilence.2014

4) "Brothers of Silence 2017".

Diagnosing Healthcare Assignments: Medical Interpreting for Deaf People in Europe

Patricia Brück, Britta Meinicke, Juliane Rode

patricia.brueck@dolmetschserviceplus.at

b.meinicke@netcologne.de

julianerode@gmail.com

Abstract:

This article presents the insights of five practicing signed language interpreters into the conditions and factors that characterize professional interpreting in the medical field in Austria and Germany. To this purpose, a total of 142 healthcare assignments, completed by the five interpreters in 2012, and 59 medical encounters in 2017, were documented and analyzed. We discuss recurrent features of medical encounters between deaf patients and hearing doctors that involve a signed language interpreter. The data presented here suggest that, more often than not, interpreters will encounter conditions that are conducive to the satisfactory outcome of healthcare assignments. We then present the results of a workshop conducted with 11 interpreters in Austria about their experiences in medical interpreting. We also add the contributions of interpreters from other European countries that had been added at the conference.

Keywords:

Health care interpreting, deaf patients, sign language, Austria, Germany

1. Introduction

This contribution presents the results of a piece of practice research on health care interpreting in Germany and Austria, conducted in 2012 and 2017, by five respectively three working interpreters and Prof. Jens Hessman from Magdeburg-Stendal University of Applied Sciences.

Furthermore, it looks into the results of a workshop conducted with the staff interpreter of a clerical hospital, Lisa Wipplinger on the same topic in Linz, Austria in spring 2017 where 11 interpreters talked about their experiences in medical interpreting. Finally, we present the contributions of the interpreters at the conference to add other countries' perspectives to justify our audacious title "Health Care Interpreting in EUROPE".

2. The study

The foundation of our study on health care interpreting was an investigation into the working experiences of five sign language interpreters in Germany and Austria conducted in 2012. For a whole year, the five interpreters did reflective logs of their medical assignments and recorded them in diary fashion; we logged basic data (e.g. patient's age and gender, medical condition, etc.), duration of assignment, number of people involved, details of each medical assignment, gave a sketch of "how it went", and also commented on non-linguistic aspects that might have helped or hindered the success of the assignment (e.g. level of familiarity amongst the patient, doctor, and interpreter; doctor's attitudes, background knowledge of the medical staff, as well as what transpired in the waiting room).

Data were organized to collectively identify various conditions that the interpreters experienced as being either supportive of or hindering to interpreter-mediated healthcare.

The main goal of this study was to enable the participating practitioners to reflect on the experience of professional sign language interpreters in the healthcare system and identify conditions that they experience as supportive of their practice as opposed to those factors that can make their work difficult or stressful. The results of this field research were published in Nicodemus and Metzger (2014).

From January to June 1917, the study was repeated to check its validity. Data were collected by three of the five interpreters of the initial study and analysed the same way as in 2012.

We kept a log of all our health care assignments. These notes were entered into a data base and evaluated with regard to ten recurring features that we considered as distinctive components of medical interpreting assignments. While the triad of patient, doctor and interpreter is at the centre of medical consultations, further components contribute to the overall progression and success of an assignment.

In 2012 we had 142 assignments with 60 different patients, in 2017 we analysed 59 assignments with 30 patients. The difference might be due to the fact that the second period is only half a year and would have been higher if we had looked into another full year as the deaf patients tend to use the same interpreter for all their health care assignments. The urgency of the assignments is generally "normal": 64% (2017: 77%), only 18% of the assignments are of high urgency (2017: 5,2%). As to the location of the medical encounters, the majority took place at doctors' offices 67,6 % (2017: 58%), only 30% (2017: 40%) at clinics.

The fact that 96% (2017: 93%) of all assignments are with medical specialists is striking. This may be due to a number of reasons, including the fact that deaf patients may prefer to use an interpreter

efsli 2017 proceedings

when seeing a specialist to avoid miscommunication but use other ways of communication with their general practitioners. In both data sets, the four main areas are gynaecology, internal medicine, paediatric care and ophthalmology although not in the same ranking and proportion.

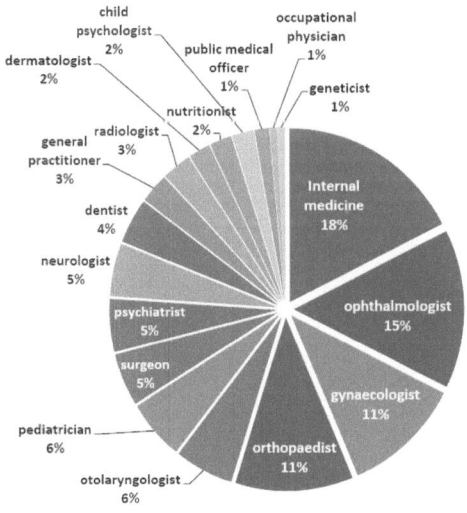

Diagram 1: medical fields of interpreted assignments in 2012

efsli 2017 proceedings

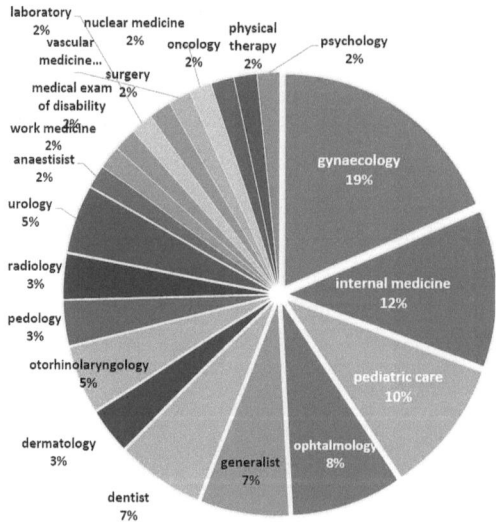

Diagram 2: medical fields of interpreted assignments in 2017

In both years, there are more women attending medical services than men, although the disproportion is really striking in the data from 2017: 22 women opposed to two men, whereas in 2012, the relation was 28:21.

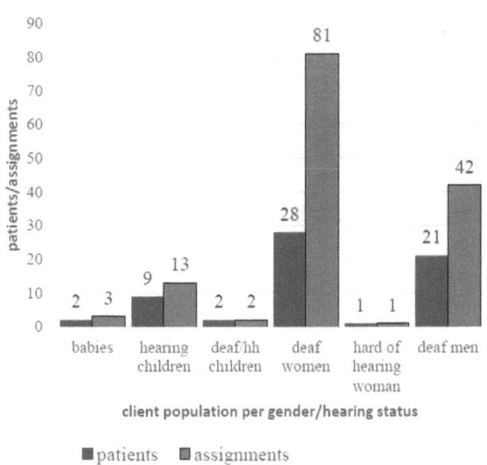

Diagram 3: patents and assignments 2012 by gender and hearing status

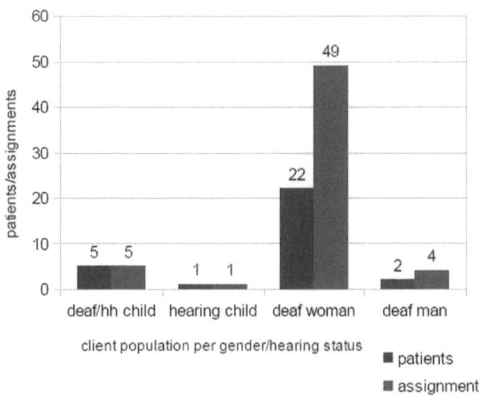

Diagram 4: patients and assignments 2017 by gender and hearing status

2.1 Results

2.1.1 Procurement

Someone has to "bring in" an interpreter. In Austria and Germany, this is done mostly by the deaf customer her/himself. They prefer to call an interpreter they trust and have known for some time. Some assignments were organized by others, such as family members, caregivers, social workers, or other sign language interpreters. Very few assignments were organized by hearing doctors or their staff.

2.1.2 Waiting room interaction

More often than not, even with an appointment, patients have to wait before they can see the doctor. This time is rarely idly spent but rather may allow for crucial interaction between deaf patients and interpreters. It is about briefing the interpreter by procuring vital information and about developing the rapport between deaf clients and interpreters.

2.1.3 Medical staff

In most cases, the initial contact at the clinic or at the doctor's office is made with a receptionist. Their attitude may have a considerable impact on the doctor's attitude and on the climate and tone of the consultation.

In more than one third (37%, 2017: 79%) of all assignments receptionists were perceived as friendly, polite and helpful by the interpreters. Some communicate directly with the client.

2.1.4 Doctors

All the doctors in this study were hearing. Obviously, their attitudes and behaviours contribute crucially to the success of the interpreted interaction. Unfortunately, the pressure on doctors exerted by institutional structures or lack of time are detrimental to the success of medical consultations. In positively rated assignments, doctors were often familiar with the overall situation and knew either the deaf patient (34,5%, 2017: 52,5%) or both the deaf patient and the interpreter (23,9%, 2017:33,9%). But respectful behaviour does not depend on familiarity; attitudes appear to be crucial, as we found some doctors unfamiliar with deaf patients or interpreters treating their patients with respect and adjusting to the patients' needs (e.g. using visual material for explanations). On the other hand, lack of empathy with the patient and disrespect made few doctors misuse the interpreter as a bearer of bad news (by asking them to explain the negative diagnosis outside of his office) or a caregiver of a patient in despair (by leaving the interpreter to deal with the emotional reaction of the deaf client).

2.1.5 Deaf Patients

All the patients in this study were deaf (including a small number of patients who might be considered hard of hearing in audiological terms). In a number of cases, deaf clients accompanied their deaf or hearing children.

We identified three main reasons for dissatisfaction with the assignment of deaf patients:

- confusion about the flow of communication and roles of people present,
- interaction that lacked explanation (e.g. a diagnosis was given without sufficient clarification), and/or
- the patients' misguided expectations (e.g. doctor did not prescribe their preferred medicine).

The interpreters considered it helpful if the patients took initiative and tried to control the communication, this included quite ordinary behaviours, such as introducing themselves and their interpreters, asking questions, etc.

Even proactive deaf patients were not always successful in their attempts to get what they wanted, and sometimes it took great assertiveness to elicit answers out of a doctor. It can be problematic if the agenda of the assignment is ignored, e.g. patients who repeatedly interrupted the doctor, or would not stop talking, even after the doctor had clearly brought the consultation to a close. Sometimes patients complained and made demands, without acknowledging that the doctor had already made an effort to accommodate their wishes. Another difficult situation arose when a deaf patient refused to cooperate with the doctor, came unprepared, questioned the usefulness of the procedure and did not accept the doctor's advice.

Occasionally, lack of signing skills or unskilled use of fingerspelling can also cause problems if the interpreter does not understand or cannot be understood by the deaf patient.

2.1.6 Interpreters

The situation may prompt interpreters to react or get involved in different ways. Generally, there is more involved than simply rendering messages. Generally, the interpreter's intervention is necessary to create suitable conditions for the interpreting tasks. Thus, the interpreter may ask for a change in the position of a chair, intervene to shorten the waiting time, or instruct medical staff about how to proceed during an examination. We found that interpreters intervened

- • when faced with ignorance on the part of a doctor or staff member concerning deaf patients or the interpreting process
- • the interpreter tried to stop patronizing or dominating behaviour by the hearing doctor or staff member

- • when s/he felt the need to advocate for the deaf customer because of the diffidence or insecurity of the deaf person in interacting with hearing people or the doctor
- • because of an inconsiderate use of technical jargon to make sure to understand the message to be conveyed.

2.2 Drawbacks

Level of detail that was recorded varied between interpreters, and in some instances, it proved difficult to verify particular aspects of the assignment from memory at a later date.

3. Workshop on Healthcare interpreting in Linz, Austria, in VI/2017

Patricia Brück, a freelance interpreter, and Lisa Wipplinger, a staff interpreter at a Clerical Hospital in Linz, conducted a workshop to look more closely into the Austrian situation. The nine participant interpreters plus the two presenters represented several federal countries; the range of individual professional interpreting experience was from 1 to 20 years. After the presentation of the study of 2012, the interpreters took a vote on the ten features of healthcare interpreting analysed in the study and chose four to be examined in more detail. The method applied was brainstorming where the interpreters were given time to put down their ideas, problems, memories on cards that were subsequently presented to the whole group and clustered on pin boards.

The four features chosen were: waiting room interaction, deaf patients, examinations/treatments, debriefing.

3.1 Waiting room

Time in the waiting room is put to good use. We attend to our customers to reduce their stress or fear, we listen to their complaints, keep the time and remind the HC staff of their deaf patient, we are briefed for the consultation, interpret forms or written explanations.

The problems mentioned were: is it my duty to make small talk or listen to complaints about foreign refugees or political parties? The privacy of a communication in sign language was questioned as more and more hearing people learn sign language.

3.2 Deaf patients

As to deaf patients, the interpreters mentioned problems that make their work difficult:

- Lack of knowledge: general, health, medical and some deaf patients do not even know their own health status
- There are deaf patients with little sign language competence and without skills in fingerspelling
- Many do not know how to properly communicate with doctors/nurses and do not know how much they should share (life story?)
- They lack a clear picture of the work of an interpreter
- Some deaf patients are a source of embarrassment for the interpreter
- And how do we not intrude into their privacy?

3.3 Examinations or treatments

When it comes to examinations or treatments, the SLI does not only interpret, but:

- Explain the situation and the needs of patients and SLI to the doctors and nurses
- Make arrangements for communication if SL cannot be used (ophthalmologist with USHER patients)
- Give support to the deaf anxious patient

The problems mentioned were position, lightning, protection of doctor or interpreter (e.g. face mask), time restrictions, and the very presence of the interpreter embarrassing the deaf patient or crowding the narrow space of the examination room.

3.4 Debriefing

When debriefing, the interpreter has to take on a lot of tasks:

- Repeating the instructions given by doctor
- Reexplaining some instructions/facts
- Organising next assignments/replacement
- Passing on of information
    there is no harm in sharing information with another free-lance interpreter as s/he is still bound by her/his professional confidentiality. It may be problematic, if the interpreter is a staff interpreter and may have to divulge information that the patient would not like to be known by the doctor who was not present at an examination or consultation with a colleague.

The problems mentioned were: the interpreter usually is no medical expert and does not feel secure when repeating the doctor's instruction or explaining medical facts. As the time of the debriefing is not considered to be part of the assignment, interpreters are usually not paid for their additional time and effort.

These results were put into a mindmap that we will provide upon request but the language used is German. There is a second part of the workshop planned for this November where we want to examine more features and explore controls to the demands identified.

4. Contributions of other European countries

Belgium

Belgium has three interpreting agencies. VRI is little used. The contributing interpreter is a staff interpreter. Being a staff interpreter has the advantage of continuity, but the disadvantage of the Deaf patient not being able to choose who is going to interpret for her/him. If staff interpreters are not available, free lancers are brought in. The contributing interpreter does not do a lot of VRI, only a small percentage (5%) of her work load, as she does not like it because of the big chance of misunderstandings.

Usually it is the deaf person bringing in the interpreter, not the doctor. The medical staff often is not informed about sign language interpreting and there is no briefing or debriefing time planned. It is possible to bring in a deaf intermediary. In the southern part of Belgium, there is good health care service with deaf intermediaries. Nevertheless, the status of deaf interpreters is unclear.

Croatia

The situation is similar to that of Austria and Germany, but interpreters are employed. When working in health care, they have to face the fact that doctors and medical staff lack patience, they expect the interpreter to explain the problem/the symptoms of the patient and not the patient her/himself.

France

There are 15 services for deaf patients providing sign language or sign language interpreting and even deaf intermediaries if needed.

The contributing interpreter reports about consultations in difficult cases like cancer patients. S/he asks the question how to find the right register for a deaf child that may be involved.

Ireland

The Irish contributor reports of problems with having no information of the gender of the patient that is not divulged by the booking agency because of confidentiality issues. There was a case of a deaf woman explicitly asking for a female interpreter but the agency sent a man. The assignment had to be referred.

Lithuania

The contributor reports about long waiting hours at health care services. The interpreters had asked the deaf association for support. They addressed the municipality responsible for health issues. These authorities have ruled that deaf people with interpreters have now priority to be admitted.

Macedonia

There are big problems in the medical area e.g. with mental health. The diagnoses of mental problems are very superficial. The deaf patients do not understand their diagnosis. The interpreters have advocated with the government for access to medical information and have explained about the short time of medical appointments as deaf people do not have enough time to explain their situation or really understand what the doctors tell them.

Norway

There is an interpreter service provided for the Deaf community. In contrast to Germany and Austria, interpreters have been instructed not to sit in the waiting room with the deaf patient. The reason for this is a research study conducted by Katharina Cecilia Williams about medical consultations. She found that Deaf people talking in the waiting room with their interpreters before the appointment did not talk to the doctor afterwards because they were expecting the interpreter to relay the information to the doctor as they had already explained everything in the waiting room.

Romania

There is a severe lack of understanding about the role of the sign language interpreter among the medical staff. The contributing deaf interpreter was working for a deaf blind mother when the doctor asked her/him to leave the room not to disturb the privacy of the patient without understanding that he had no way of communicating without the interpreter being present.

UK

Deaf patients cannot choose their interpreters as interpreters are booked by agencies who do not respect the deaf customers' needs or wishes (e.g. the same interpreter for follow-up appointment). They often do not convey enough or complete information e.g. the preferred gender or the department (problem with informed choices – not all interpreters like to take mental health appointments). Sometimes the interpreters are not informed about the name of the patient (possible conflicts of interest!). Sometimes scarce interpreter resources are wasted because two departments of the same hospital book interpreters for the same day. Some agencies have been known to engage untrained, unregistered and unqualified interpreters for health care settings.

What has been presented here are only glimpses into an important and delicate area of sign language interpreting in Europe. We are convinced that it is high time to look into health care interpreting in more detail and we would very much like to see more research into the practice of other European countries. We believe that providing successful sign language interpreting is one of the most important means to give deaf people access to knowledge about health issues and health care in general.

What has been presented here are only glimpses into an important and delicate area of sign language interpreting in Europe. We are convinced that it is high time to look into health care interpreting in more detail and we would very much like to see more research into the practice of other European countries. We believe that providing successful sign language interpreting is one of the most important means to give deaf people access to knowledge about health issues and health care in general.

5. References

Brueck, P., Rode, J., Hessmann, J., Meinicke, B., Unruh, D., & Bergmann, A., Diagnosing Healthcare Assignments: A Year of Medical Interpreting for Deaf People in Austria and Germany (2014). In: Nicodemus, B. and Metzger, M. (eds.), Investigations in Healthcare Interpreting, Washington: Gallaudet University Press, 128-184.

Contributors to this presentation:

Patricia Brueck, Britta Meinicke, Juliane Rode

Patricia Brück earned an M.A. Degree in Sign Language Interpreting (EUMASLI) after having completed her interpreting studies for spoken languages in the 1980s (Master of Philosophy). After having worked in different areas, she completed her education as a sign language interpreter. She has been working as a professional sign language interpreter for more than 14 years. Her area of expertise is educational interpreting from secondary level through vocational training to university lectures, conference interpreting, and political settings. Her academic interest lies in team interpreting, gender issues in interpreting, health care interpreting, and the ethics of the profession.

Britta Meinicke has been working as a certified German Sign Language interpreter since 2005. She participated in the first round of EUMASLI and got an M.A. degree in Sign Language Interpreting in 2011. After studying French, Russian and agricultural economy and 10 years of working in economic research about Eastern Europe, she learned Sign Language out of curiosity and - fascinated by discovering the Deaf world - decided to change profession. Britta also works with GIB Zeit, an organisation where Deaf adults teach sign language to hearing parents and their deaf children in order to help them communicate.

Juliane Rode earned a Diploma in Sign Language Interpreting in 2003 and has been working as an sign language interpreter focusing on vocational training, university lectures, and community interpreting, ever since. She participated in the first round of the EUMASLI finishing with an M.A. degree in 2011. Since 2016 she has been lecturing at the University of Applied Science in Landshut.

www.ingramcontent.com/pod-product-compliance
Lightning Source LLC
Chambersburg PA
CBHW040220240426
43662CB00030BA/29